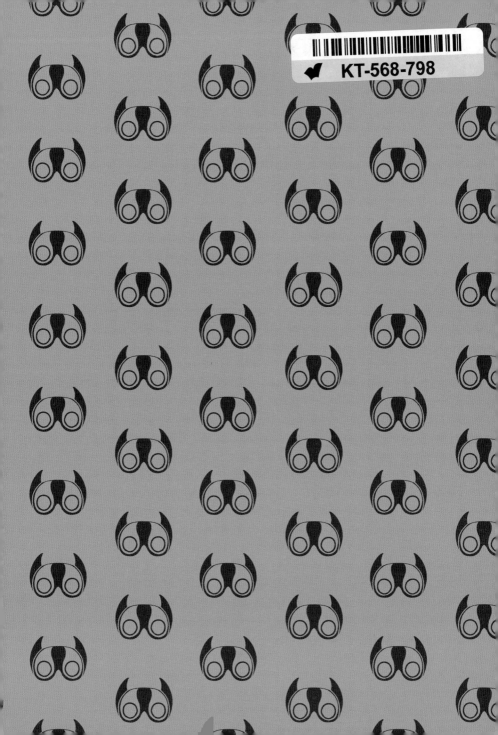
KT-568-798

ALEKSANDR ORLOV

PRESENTS

ALEKSANDR
& THE MYSTERIOUS
KNIGHTKAT

**MEERKAT CLASSICS**

RUSSIA 2012

Aleksandr & the Mysterious Knightkat
**ALEKSANDR ORLOV**

3 5 7 9 10 8 6 4 2

First published in 2012 by Ebury Press, an imprint of Ebury Publishing

A Random House Group company

Copyright © **compare**the**meerkat**.com 2012

**compare**the**meerkat**.com has asserted its right to be identified as the author
of this Work in accordance with the Copyright, Designs and Patents Act 1988

This is an advertisement feature on behalf of **compare**the**market**.com

**compare**the**meerkat**.com and **compare**the**market**.com
are trading names of BISL Limited

All rights reserved. No part of this publication may be reproduced, stored in
a retrieval system, or transmitted in any form or by any means, electronic,
mechanical, photocopying, recording or otherwise, without the prior
permission of the copyright owner

The Random House Group Limited Reg. No. 954009

Addresses for companies within the Random House Group can be found at
www.randomhouse.co.uk

A CIP catalogue record for this book is available from the British Library

The Random House Group Limited supports The Forest Stewardship Council
(FSC®), the leading international forest certification organisation. Our
books carrying the FSC label are printed on FSC® certified paper. FSC is
the only forest certification scheme endorsed by the leading environmental
organisations, including Greenpeace. Our paper procurement policy can be
found at www.randomhouse.co.uk/environment

Printed and bound in Italy by Graphicom SRL

ISBN 9780091950026

To buy books by your favourite authors and register for offers visit
www.randomhouse.co.uk

This is a work of fiction. Names and characters are the product of the
author's imagination and any resemblance to actual persons, living or dead,
is entirely coincindental

# A MESSAGE FROM THE AUTHOR

Welcome to my bookamabob!

I think you are opening this very special volume with feeling of great excitement. It is the true story of a superhero told by me, Aleksandr.

You already know me as star of stage and screen and semi-successful theatre directings. Now you are see me as writer of literary storytellings!

It has everything you could want in a storytelling: Suspense! Actions! Huge bravenesses! And very importantly a hero of great handsomeness.

Now. Please turn over page and begin…

Yours,

*Aleksandr*

ALEKSANDR ORLOV

PS: There is hiding in text arithmetic puzzle!
It is on page 20. Answer is at back of book.

# It was dark
# and stormy night.

In mountain village of Meerkovo everywhere was full of
raining, and the wind made rattle against the window panes.
The sign of the Queasy Mongoose tavern creak and squeak in
the howling gale. Everyone was glad to be tucked up in bed.

They didn't know that not far away, in **Orlov** family mansion, there was one who never sleep.

Deep in the heart of the house, behind library and underneath ballroom, was secret dungeon of great enormousness. It was full of flashing computermabobs... and rockets... and super-charged sports cars...

This is south side of Orlov family mansion.
The three giant trees were grown from seed by my Great Granddaddy Vitaly and completely block out light in library!

In the middle of it all were two figures.
One was handsome and furry and wearing
a red gown. The other was small and grey
and scratching himself.

The handsome one was sip his ladybird tea
and **thinking great thoughts.**\*
The grey one was trying to mend his
Walkman, in between picking out
the fleas from behind his ears.

\*We do not know exactly what
these thoughts were but we can
be sure they were great.

This was secret lair of **Knightkat**, superhero of all Russia, and deadly enemy of evil **Doctor Robogoose**, the cruellest mongoose villain in the world. (He get his name because he half robot, half mongoose, which make him stinky metal scoundrel).

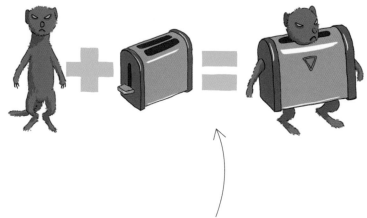

*Illustration of science principle: fur+metal=villain.*
*(Do not take it literals; if you put a mongoose in a toaster a stinky metal villain does not pop out).*

Suddenly there was buzzing noise of great urgency. Knightkat (for it is he) nearly spilt his tea on his cravat. The biggest computer was flash and beep and make great alarm.

"Alert!
    Alert!
        Alert!"

It say in computer voice.

"Maiya.
    Danger.
        Danger."

On the screen was picture from Knightkat's secret camera which could show Knightkat all the streets of Moscow at once. (Sometimes Knightkat use it to see where traffic jams, but mostly he use it to save world). Now it show a scene of great frighteningness.

On roof of Presidential Palace in centre of Moscow was evil **Doctor Robogoose**. Dangling from his evil claw was helpless figure of beautiful **Princess Maiya**.

# She had been kidnap!

*Here is beautiful Maiya. I look at this picture often –*
*I am sure her wink is for me!*

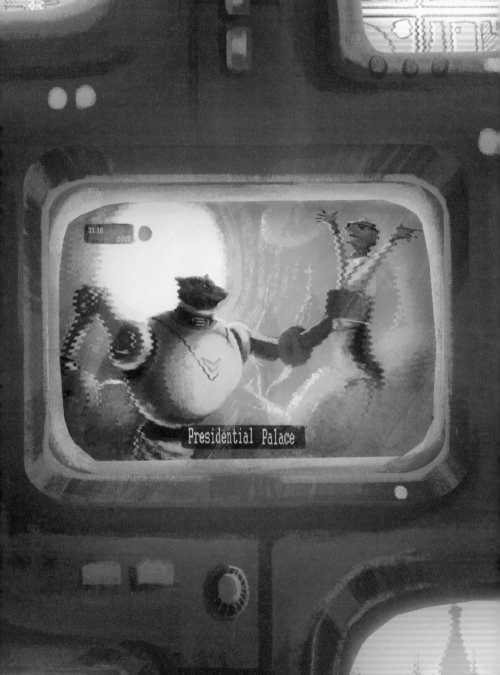

"This is case for Knightkat," said Knightkat.*

Before you could say "costumed crusader"
Knightkat was wearing his Turbo-Charged
Flying Cape and his 3-D Night Vision Mask,
and was standing in the Knightkat
Ejector Lift.

*Like all very famous peoples he
use third person when he talk of
himself. Is sign of superhero and
not bad grammar.

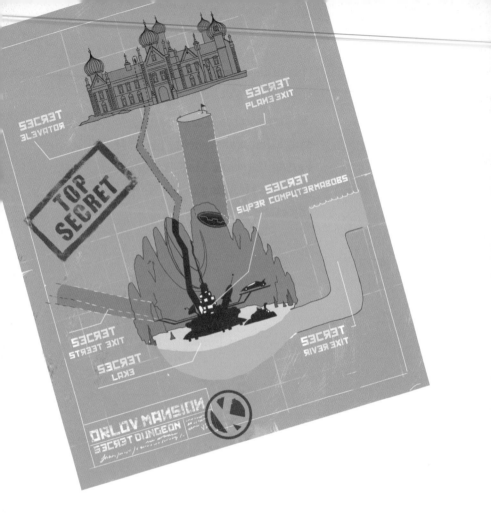

With a loud whooooooooosh that knock small grey figure off his feet, the Knightkat Ejector Lift shot Knightkat up on roof of mansion.

There, lighting up stormy dark sky was brilliant sign.
## It was Knightkat sign!
It show world that Knightkat was on a mission.

Miles away in Meerkovo the bright light of Knightkat's sign woke everyone up. When they saw the sign, they say to each other: "It is Knightkat on a mission. Something dreadful must be happen". And they turned on their computermabobs to see what it could be.

# Unfortunately the computermabobs is **CLOG**!

So they decide to go back to sleep and wait till morning.

Meanwhile, Knightkat
sniffed the air, leaned into
howling gale and swooped
off roof and into the dark.*

15 Sec.

10 Sec

5 Sec.

KNIGHTKAT
LAIR

*Do not try this at home. Without special equipment
you will go splat on ground and be messy.

19

20 Sec

25 Sec

30 Sec

PR3SID3NTIAL
PALAC3
16.66 MIL3S

It was very fast swoop; his **Turbo-Charged Flying Cape** make him travel at 2000 miles an hour, so he get to roof of Presidential Palace in only thirty seconds.

*(Can you work out distance Knightkat fly to palace?)*

There he discover hideous sight.

# Doctor Robogoose was clutch poor Princess Maiya by her waist!

She was frozen in astonish and fright. The evil Robogoose was making roaring noise into the night, and waving the Princess's crown in triumphant.

Knightkat have to act quick before all is lost.*

Here we see how evil Dr Robogoose's hands are FILL with nastiness – but I think he is missing tin opener!

*This is extra thrillsy moment.
Music will go thumpy bumpy in film version.

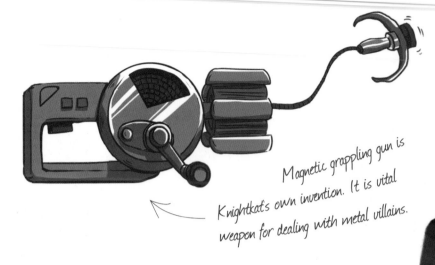

Magnetic grappling gun is Knightkat's own invention. It is vital weapon for dealing with metal villains.

He dive towards the wicked Robogoose and using his specials **Magnetic Grappling Gun** he fire the hook round leg of evil monster.

With all his strength **Knightkat** pull **Robogoose** off balance and he is hurling him into the darkness below. As he fall, **Knightkat** scoop **Maiya** into his arms.

It all happen very fast, and Maiya is breathless.

"You are safe now," Knightkat whisper to her. He felt her heart tremble against his. And he see how the wind make patterns in her beautiful soft fur. As he flies off with her in his arms he is feeling a little trembly himself.

As he puts her gently down Maiya reaches up to him, moves his mask aside and is looking lovingly at her rescuer.

"Aleksandr......"

The voice was not so soft. In fact, the voice wasn't soft at all.

It was all raspy and – it was Sergei!

At that moment, Aleksandr woke up. He find himself in his special Cravat Room and see Sergei looking up at him.

Sergei was looking all puzzlement. But Aleksandr drew himself to his full height (which was very high due to aristocraticness), and in instant became the entrepreneur businesskat and master of Orlov family mansion again.

His secret identity as saver of the world was secret still.

# Aleksandr's Life Lesson

If you are force of evil and made of metal, you will be getting your comeuppance from force of good, made of fur.

#Extra mark for swotkat who know that Presidential Palace is 16.6 miles from Orlov family mansion!

# Now read my other greatest tales

## Available from all good bookshops

Also available to download as an ebookamabob
or audiomajig as read by the author – me!

For more information visit www.comparethemeerkat.com

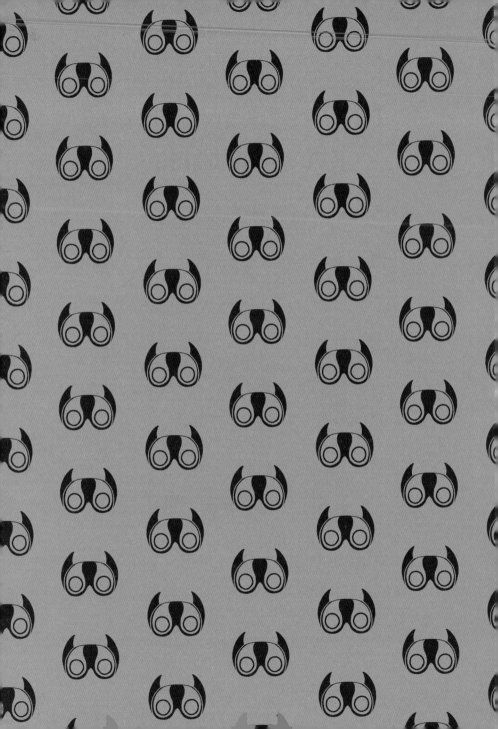